THE PATH OF A BRAVE KING

By: Alex R. Zackery

Acknowledgments

Through the journey of creating this guide of gems, I have received a great deal of support and inspiration.

I would first like to thank my most high creator for the ability to create and transcend in life.

I would like to acknowledge my mother and father for allowing me to breathe the air of this life. Your bravery, love, and guidance is cherished forever.

I would also like to thank my Malkia and watoto. Your true love and amazing encouragement has most definitely motivated me to persevere and achieve higher accolades. The name of our royal legacy will flow through our creations. The trail of God's aura we share will live and thrive forever.

Never down play the level you are on. KEEP IT UP THERE.

**Each day lay a brick.
Brick roads lead to GOLD castles.**

**Every day time passes.
Hopefully you will the test.**

The madness is only an illusion your only conclusion is GRIND.

When they double back prices go up!

Cash is a great TOOL, but you can definitely tell them to pay you in crypto currency.

Different time zones means different money, different opportunities, as well as different frequencies. MOVE AROUND!

Risk the business for elevation.

Whatever you want, add your dedication.

Peep what's REAL and what's FRAUD.

KING ME!

QUEEN ME!

CROWN ME I AM A GOD!

Wear your crown however you desire.

Brave Souls come from the most high.

You are directly connected to the Most High. Tap into self and you'll tap into the MOST HIGH.

Success and failure are both free CHOOSE ONE.

Reputation of success leaves Legacies.

BeBrave on your life journey. Everything you need is already possessed within.

Be LOVING and GENTLE with your SPIRIT, it Belongs to a Greater Purpose.

Brand yourself with the aura of infinity.

Have true, genuine, foreseen conversations with yourself. You already somehow know your truth.

Your truth is your beginning and your ending.

Fight the obstacles and you will win. Only LESSONS never loses.

STEP or FALL forward either way it's forward.

Freedom is a birthright therefore it's priceless.

Tomorrow is a new LIFE.

Every time the sunrise you get another CHANCE.

TAP INTO it Super Saiyan EXECUTE a plan.

Dig deep and POLISH GEMS.

You're walking around with your DREAMS.

Jars of clay that contain the RICHES in which you search.

Ask the Most High to reveal and illuminate your path.

The POWER to CREATE is yours. What are you creating?

Wolf your pack and hunt for tomorrow.

Never bow to the oppression of the oppressor.
Even if it's you.

**Peace is priceless.
How much do you
have to give?**

BIG shit happens to BIG DOERS.

BIG DREAMS come to BIG DREAMERS.

Always feed the people.

The song of the struggle will change overtime.

Make sure you surround yourself with a successful frequency.

Keep your aura HIGH.

Empowerment is a torch. Keep it lit.

The sky is you. Same above as below. Same inner same outer.

**Don't take it personal.
The story has to be
written.**

Write your own news clip.

Shine as bright as you desire.

Kings of Nations eat together.

**Queens make moves
Kings can't.**

Use your words wisely.

War is the result of EGO.

POWER isn't always loud.

POWER isn't alway bright.

POWER isn't always big.

Power is control.

What do you control?

Choose your Queen wisely. She will either enhance
or destroy your EMPIRE.

Choose your King wisely. He will with either exalt you or he will domesticate you.

Grow powerful young Queen.

Grow powerful young KING.

Enjoy the fruits of your labor.

Your fruits have seeds, plant them and receive more.

Tend to your garden.

Be TRUE, Be YOU!

Be full of courage, you will need it.

DIE EMPTY!!!

Transcend with Nations feed with your soul.

Study all your DEMONS.
Like a nerd or some.

You are amazing beyond your wildest dreams.

Desire your creator's voice.

**Eyes to the hills you will see your help.
Close your
eyes and see the truth.**

The walking dead isn't you. AWAKE!!!

If it is well with your soul it is true.

Make your moves in a righteous light KING.

Make your moves in a righteous light QUEEN.

Would you rather be called QUEEN or GODDESS?

Would you be a radical if your legacy depended on it?

Would you rather be called KING or GOD?

The way you walk has a great invisible influence young King.

The way you talk has great influence young Queen.

Honor thyself by your actions and contributions.

Be proud of your CREATIONS.

Higher learning is a MUST.

**There is always pain.
Use is as fuel GOD.**

**There is always pain.
Use is as fuel
GODDESS.**

**You are eating what?
You are.**

Eat fruits of the SUN.

You will need the energy to achieve greatness.

Change your mind, body, soul to reflect greatness, which you are.

Bondage starts in the mental, and works its way through the spin.

When you're drained, use the rain water.

Allow the rain to fall on your grave, for a ROSE shall grow.

GOD MIND getting clearer. ENJOY.

Keep it playa.

Get your GRIND ON.

Get your SHINE ON.

Keep striving for greatness!

Seeds have been
planted in your soul,
DON'T let
them rot.

**You will most definitely reap what you sow.
What are you sewing?**

Plan for the future.

**Plant for the future
your seeds deserve it.**

Omnipresence is yours to conquer.

If you want it go get it.

Who will follow your tracks of success?

Protect your life with your life! It's your life.

Stand on your morals with RESPECT and HONOR.

Proper discipline will lead to your greatest peaks and victories on your journey.

You posse the power to defy gravity.

Either you are going to do it for yourself, or you are going to do it for someone else.

Fear is an illusion that kills if you allow it. BeBrave and kiss fear with so much passion that you get destiny pregnant.

What is inspiration?
It's an invisible force
that attracts towards
its gravitational pull.
(force)

What is dedication? The ability to surpass and be of continuous force in a precise direction,

Grounded and humble two different words. Being humble is a more dormant mindset. Being grounded means you have the ability to POWER UP at any time due to your balance. The future holds abundance to those who seek
and prepare for it.

Like energy attracts like energy. In the process of mastering your energy, you feel uncomfortableness.

Elevation is upon those that are. In which direction are you choosing to EVOLVE.

A purpose is appointed to each whom assumes responsibility.

Your POWER is your POWER. To whom, where, and why will it be applied? Are you drained or Replenished with your relations and activities?

Before destruction always lies warnings. How often do you run red lights and roll through STOP signs?

You will learn a lot of RULES alone the way. Some are solid some are an illusion which ones will you break, create and abide by young Gods and Goddess?

**The Empire is yours.
How will you rule
before
and after life?**

Crowds aren't always the right path. Make sure your spirit of discernment stays sharp.

Guide our tribe to springs of life.

They will follow you to success or destruction. You hold that POWER.

Success is based upon your judgement. BE BRAVE in all angles of your pyramid.

Look at your fingers. Now look at your fingerprints. What have you created?

A King standing on solid principles will out far shine a peasant with diamonds. BE BRAVE.

BE BRAVE Love freely and with passion of honors. It WILL return to GOD which sent it 100 fold.

Gather and harvest your energy. It is a gift to protect or spread accordingly.

Which such distant to conquer? How will you sleep? How will you dream? How will you manifest?

Instinct is POWERFUL listen as you tread through the trenches.

Your peace of mind will remain if you handle your business. If you have no business there will
be no peace.

Queens are the most vicious pieces on the board, RESPECT that.

Kings can coexist find your land and build with RESPECT, PRINCIPLES, and LOVE.

Love is the spirit of God, the most high. Make sure you eat of it daily.

Embrace a fools knowledge on self destruction. You can learn unlimited lessons in his history.

BeBrave in ruling your Empire, for the world relies on your moves.

In order to respond to any given situation, you must 1st know your true self.

Take your wisdom, understanding and knowledge for face value.

Absorb life, embrace life, for it is a precious gift from a Goddess/Queen.

Worry less and keep moving forward. Everything will reveal itself in divine time.

Stand tall and firm, you were a warrior since before birth.

Nothing about GOD is weak.

The future awaits the. Unless it's your final destination.

No one can escape life alive. It is a must that you imprint your spirit in the wind.

All invisible outweighs the physical, beware of what you do in the dark.

Your kingdom must have UNITY. Lead by POWERFUL example.

Document your life, so that your lineage will never forget (his)tory.

A clear thought process is needed on the battlefield. Beware of cloudy rivers (your mind).

Your natural desire for Queens is naturally your birthright. RESPECT that POWER, which you possess.

You can judge your performance in life by the standards of the impact on your family, community, and purpose.

Be fully engaged in your doings, most things you do will impact the way your steps are aligned.

The Evolution of you having offspring needs your legacy to continue. Nurture your spirits.

Allow your desire and edge for life to be a powerful weapon of your amour.

Nobody may understand your moves or your vision at the moment, it's okay. Keep Grinding.

The more you control yourself the more forceful your moves will be.

The force of your force must be maintained at its strongest.

Arise to every occasion, that is why you possess a greater POWER.

Study the great element called water, your adult body is 60% of it.

Wherever there is great energy there will be trickles of that source.

He who speaks life will attract Life.

He who speaks death will for-sure attract destruction.

Wisdom that is always kept to self is always wisdom wasted.

Poverty will follow you all the days of your life and your kids' life if economicals are not obtained.

Create your own playing fields. Who said you have to play the other GAME anyway?

**The truth will always be beautiful when you take
it and apply it.**

Be prepared to receive what you work and seek for.

What are your strengths? Use and sharpen them so they will be of good use.

Confront and acknowledge your weaknesses. Ignoring them is the way of the weak.

BeBrave life will ask for the most of you along your journey.

Handling your business and building your legacy gives you the right to wear your crown however you want. Apply your style.

Through your life's journey make sure you pick up the weapon of patience. It is a guarantee you will need it countless times.

Throughout your life's journey always take care of your spaceship (your body), you only get one.

Your ability to battle will highly be based upon your previous practices and expenses.

You can always get material possessions back.
You can never get your time back, magnify what you do.

Accept which is only True and Righteous to you.

Radical Kings change the world. Dormant mentality is not that route.

You live and you learn, it's even kill.
Choose
your kill wisely.

Without patience our plans and moves will fail. Only the BRAVE will weather the storm

Pay attention to the Greater Vision. The petty has no place in your future.

Surround yourself with people that appreciate "YOU".

It's here for you to enjoy. Cherish no possessions.

Anger and emotions can be used in a very efficient way, if learned how to control.

Putting your pants on one leg at a time means you're aware of your ability to wear the pants. Now take one step at a time and walk into YOUR GREATNESS. BE BRAVE.

Spend time as if it's an investment in your next life, for tomorrow is a new life.

Your network will dictate how far your bankroll will reach. Take these flights and mingle.

If you can't count you can't add, if you can't add you can't multiple. Make sure you learn the basics.

The Most High Creator wants you to be the head and not the tail. Who is the head of your life?

Walk as a King and own the ground you walk on.

Train your mind, body, and soul. Training is a sport of God's.

It's cool to own lakes but imagine if you own rivers. Keep your waters flowing with life.

Study the GREATS before you and put YOUR OWN CREATIVITY to tracks of success.

When you paint make sure you paint your picture.

How far will your vision take you?

Great Kings fill BIG shoes.

Complicate simple things and you will overthink.

BRAVE Kings simply complicated formulas.

Honesty rest upon the crowns of Kings.

The grass is higher in the grassland because it's waiting on you to plow and create.

Mediocre actions will lead to a mediocre life. Guard your actions as if your life depended on them.

**When tough times arise always look to your left,
right, front and back.**

**Work smart, simplify complicated work to achieve High Quality Success.
It's Pros and Cons to everything you do. Always
weigh your options.**

You can engineer your direction being a creator. Never lose that small still voice within.

Press forward even if the lights go out in the hallway.

Every action has a reaction, energy never dies.

Win, lose or draw. Regardless of the odds, make up your mind and stick with it.

Whatever you envision in your mind as yourself, will most likely manifest into your physical realm.

We are all candles looking to inspire or to be inspired. BeBrave and continue to let your light shine bright. Sincerely the inspiration inside you.

Never allow the fears of yesterday to paralyze you. Today is a gift directly from The Most High given of air. For tomorrow is a new life.

Every dog has its day to bury his bones. I'm grateful that you are enlightened by words. May great peace, joy, and love be unto your BRAVE
Heart.

Watch your thoughts, they hold weight too.

Soul searching requires stillness, oneness, and patience. Learn to flow within your being. Row your boat gently. Dream big life is but it.

RESPECT takes you places money can't. Respect takes you places private jets can't. Make sure you take RESPECT with you as a shield of life through the airs, waters, and villages.

**Focus on your crown
KING and QUEEN. A
dimension may come
where you have to
pass it on
to your lineage.**

Every brick laid will take you to a new dimension, train your mind, body and spirit to
crave elevation. You will be surprised at how much Bravery God instilled in you the level before.

No excuses Kings and Queens, make it happen.
If you can see it you can do it. Grind day and night time.

Dot your Is and cross your Ts so you can sleep better at night. HANDLE YOUR BUSINESS.

BeBrave when acting on your vision. It's your
vision. Press forward and accept responsibility.

**BeBrave when it comes to love! Past traumas
are just that past.**

A King of his word is a King of POWER. Maintain your integrity, it will take you places riches can't.

It's amazing what you can do when you be you. Just do you.

Pay attention to the little signs a lot of them are preparation and inspiration. BE BRAVE!

PALY DREAMS not numbers.

Cherish no possessions; all materials are subject to GODs.

To achieve your highest dreams you need your BEST team. Find your dream team.

Energy doesn't lie.
The Sun is the Sun
and the
Moon is the Moon.

When a war is waged
a King bombs first
and
doesn't miss.

A true King must OVERstand that his words have the POWER to speak Life and Death, Abundance, and Lack. Choose wisely.

The path of Great Kings will be studied by many, but the way of a fool can save lives. Discernment is a fool.

A Brave King never lets anyone place their burdens of fear upon his soul.

With one stroke at a time, paint your vision, goals and life.

Honor your physical form, for it is your transportation to your next destination.

A Brave King builds enterprises around his talents. The fruits will be for generations to come.

Peace be upon the BRAVE King that holds his vision even if the world is at war with him.
BeBrave.

A BRAVE King must write his name below his vision amongst the pyramid walls. I am that I am. BeBrave.

A BRAVE King must be aware of the invisible forces that work around him for his words and actions shall stay righteous.

Stand BRAVE Kings and Queens all things are working for your greater greatness. Trust the process.

A BRAVE King must stay away from demobilizing thoughts, actions, and company. Beware of destruction snares.

Waste no innerG on things of destruction, you have legacies and pyramids to build.

A BRAVE King always sets his new standards above his old ones because he knows he has more to give.

With each stroke of the pen a Brave King and Queen will write down his and her way to GREATNESS.

Never only be grounded by fear. The sky is where your name will be written. Dream BIGGER.

A BRAVE King should always indulge in ways to sharpen his sword. Why no advance? BeBrave.

A BRAVE King has everything he needs within him to achieve every goal he sets for himself. That's how he is able to see it in the first place.

A BRAVE King is never threatened by opposition that may oppose his dreams because he moves as if the vision is already complete.

A BRAVe God and Goddess accepts every UP and Down that comes with the journey to
fulfillment.

Make excuses or make it happen. There is no in between a King is firm on his decisions and positions.

You are the captain of your plane BRAVE King.
BeBrave.

King fear no oppression for war is only part of self preservation. Meet words with words, swords
with swords, fire with fire. (LINGO)

Knowledge is POWER, but only when you know how to utilize it. How are you utilizing your knowledge? - Goddess Ashley

Shifting from flesh and blood into a creator, into a God is a process that takes place within.

Hold fast to your dreams and visions. Stay strong and keep going towards what you see fit for you and your legacy.

If you don't take action you fail. Actions require faith. JUMP!

**You will have setbacks.
You will fail. Major
comebacks come to
those who fight back.
When
you fall, fall forward.**

Dreaming and using your imagination is how you bend this universe and time travel. NEVER STOP DREAMING. Never stop using your imagination.

The more discipline and organization a King and Queen has the better and faster the empire gets built.

Out of the dog shit a flower will emerge. Never quit on yourself Gods and Goddesses.

Through perseverance you will build mental, physical, and spiritual endurance.

Momentum can go 2 ways, make sure you stay on a positive frequency and keep going.

The Power and Discipline it takes to resist poverty… BRAVERY

**BeBrave and do the uncomfortable things when working towards your goals. Bang it out now
and be guaranteed to celebrate later.**

You are in charge of your ecosystem. Make the BRAVE decision to eat better. You are what you
eat. Electricity is life. Corps is death.

There is an enormous difference between thinking you are a king and knowing you are a King.

There is a gigantic difference between thinking you are a GOD, than knowing you are a GOD. It's levels to it.

BE BRAVE and take the hill. Therefore you will be the King/Queen of that hill.

Pay attention to the flashes of lights. Everything
that glitters isn't gold, and everything that looks like it is for you may not be.

Distractions are all around you, they come to steal, kill, and destroy your peace, dreams and momentum. BE BRAVE and stay the course you're almost there.

A BRAVE King realizes that he has two lives.
His second life starts when he realizes he has one life to build his empire and legacy.

Too many options to self destruct is a tyrant. BeBrave and dismiss what you are not. This method enhances your distance to successful goals.

Make it a great habit to open your mind to different books. Broaden your horizon.

LOVE your life it is a gift to open and expand to your highest depths. BeBRAVE.

With every inch worked towards YOUR success, take PRIDE and do it with foresight of looking back being proud of your work.

You may not always see eye to eye with your team. Work and talk through your differences.

Make sure you prepare yourself for your journey in whichever climates you choose to endure.

Never be ashamed of being full of intellect. Intelligence is a master tool. Use it.

Find your pace towards your goal. Don't allow your stride to be broken by fatigue. BeBRAVE.

The more focused a King's drive is the faster he can manifest what he needs into the physical dimension.

When you speak make sure you speak with words of truth, care, and purpose. Words guide, lead, tear down and build.

Keep your source of POWER, of belief inside your dimension. The enemy will never be able to use you against you.

All truth already exists inside man. Never do they live in the material things around him. TAP IN.

A true King never reveals his every move. Seem weak when you are strong. BE strong when you are weak.

A true King knows a true Queen by the way his spirit is changed by her feminine aura.

You can and will be tested by the fires of life BRAVE Kings and Queens. Show everything you've learned in your training.

BeBRAVE and always strive to take your legacy to the NEXT level. Give the young GODS
and GODDESS
coming after a HIGHER level of GREATNESS, and CONSCIOUSNESS to strive for.

START IT AND FINISH IT. Make sure to be pure and true to your vision.

With each step towards your GREATNESS, be compassionate with yourself. Enjoy your ups and downs. Life is like a roller coaster. BeBRAVE.

Each twist and turn in life's roller coaster with excitement of life itself. Absorb it GOD with admiration on your quest to the afterlife.

Life amongst the Kings is a King's thinking game. Kings build with each other.

Each King must build his throne one diamond at a time. Each gram of gold must be tested and shaped perfectly in the fire of excellence. To each King his own.

Give yourself time to breath on your marathon. Be not anxious for the finish line, but BeBRAVE enough to fight through the fatigue and climates of the invisible.

Each King will shine in his own birth right and birth light. All praise due to The Most High.

**BeBRAVE in the challenge of life. Once you
see it's all one big battle you will find it.**

Tough times DON'T last. BRAVE intelligent Kings do.

As a BRAVE King, as an entity, as a being, you have the right to protect and defend your innerG (energy).

To quit on yourself is to give in to self destruction. BeBRAVE and slay the demon of all lower vibrational energies.

Life sometimes has spilt screens in between dimensions. One side your past, one side the best life you could imagine. BeBRAVE.

Create a place where you can balance out and meditate. A well balanced and direct mind.

**Misery loves companionship. Don't waddle and
waste time with idle misery. It's all cerebral.**

BRAVE King and Queen have gratitude within your vision. Magical energies dwell within you that will be manifested every time the sun rises.

The way of a BRAVE King is not caught up in his past traumas or dramas. He is at peace with his past and moves forward in a thriving force of The Most High.

A BRAVE King even studies the trees and sees that they may shed leaves in a season, and that the shedding is only preparation for the fruitful season ahead. A life force is stored in the core of the tree for brighter manifestation.

Hair defying gravity is manifestation of a higher power. THINK SUPER NATURAL.

PEOPLE+ POWER=PROGRESS
When pushed with force and direction in a progressive light.

A King that allows his thinking to become dogmatic will surely find his kingdom at a stand still.

A True BRAVE King never puts all of his riches in one investment. Multiple streams of riches is his lifestyle.

Always remember BRAVE King, your focus creates the perception of your reality.

Basketball before the 3 point line had less boundaries. What would be your shot choice?

**If you don't like the station change the channel.
When life gets hard, never turn off the radio.**

You are ROYALTY! Never allow yourself to be placed under the dictator's thumb.

Life is a BRAVE game of skill, timing, and position. Learn and develop your skills. Allow opportunities to survive the opportunist.

aLwAys investigate information given. Do your own due diligence. Trust no-ones information but your own.

Always tend to your land. Snakes could be lurking in your grass.

A BRAVE King must live his life to the fullest fullest. No stone unturned, no mountain unclaimed, no river uncrossed.

You can lead them to the gold mine but you can't make everyone dig. BeBRAVE and put in your due diligence.

Make sure your vision aligns with your actions.
If a King doesn't see a clear path, how can he lead his people to a higher purpose?
BOSS UP.

Never forget your foundation. But also never loss sight of the goals you set for yourself. Achieve them all.

Allow the sun to charge the gold around your crown and neck. Allow the moon to sooth your fire.

Faith in your transition will determine how many seeds you plant along the way from being a Prince into a BRAVE KING.

Everything you do, do it at the best of your ability. Only you know how much Royalty pumps through your veins.

No need to live dormant, when finding yourself walks with you, and sleeps within. When you find yourself only then will you find your true wealth.

As a BRAVE King it's imperative that you care with extra abundance with those you love and entrust with your being.

When you set yourself and your heirs up with true wealth, the world is yours. BeBRAVE.

Once you realize how POWERFUL your BLACKNESS (melanin) is you will activate into a consciousness of GREATNESS, and move as the BRAVE King or Queen you are meant to be.

Young Kings are always looking up to the current Kings. The future Queens are always looking up to the current Queens. Always give them nothing less than Royalty to aspire to.

Your hair has the ability to absorb information from the sun and the rest of the universe, allow it to
flow through your golden spirals. You are the universe.
BeBRAVE.

Learn of your physical universe around you. For example Fluorite jewelry is known to help neutralize and absorb negative energy that may come into your energy field.

Take time to make time for the things that serve your greater purpose. It's your time and purpose that helps drive you forward.

When a BRAVE King reaches a certain stage of maturity, he must leave Prince level things behind him. Elevation is key.

Before you can give your value to the world effectively, you must 1st know your value of self.

As a BRAVE King you should always do great business and tie together great connections, they will always double back to you.

Building YOUR OWN EMPIRE is always more valuable than someone giving you value.

Real love will alway drive away hate. Never be consumed by the darkness that lurks for your destruction.

Rely on your greatness within and always give thanks to The Most High Creator for that strength.

The vibrations of your positive mind, words, and action will also help guide you toward your greatness.

Never allow the things of the outer realm affect the frequency you are operating on.

Everyone is not you and that is your power. Use that to your greatest benefit. Make sure that you eat
and haven enough for your harvest.

Use the energy on the inner to manifest the environment closely around you.

Holding a true position of POWER will require morals, values, and principles. Make sure that you set your mind at the best interest for your Empire
to prevail.

Beware of too much rest. Keep your physical frequency HIGH as well. Your physical strength is needed to climb at great altitude. Too much rest can create a habit of lack.

A child is a code of the universe protect the mind, body, and soul from foul play of the physical world.

Never limit your tool box. If you only have a hammer you can only solve nail problems. Stay
sharp and well rounded.

A flea can trouble a dog more than a dog can trouble a flea. Get rid of infestations at 1st notice.

Dead knowledge is worse than a burning library.
Never cease to give away gems of wisdom
and knowledge to the Royalty to come after.

As Royalty we desire to give our lineage two things. One is knowledge of self/roots, the other is knowledge of thriving/wings to soar above the world.

**Being a BRAVE King, your aura is like a mountain of strength and inspiration to the tribe.
Always plant your feet on solid grounds.**

As a BRAVE King your decision making has to be as sharp as your swords. To far to the right is destruction, to far to the left is lack of. But right in
the middle is the road to great Wealth and Prosperity.

Never take your opportunities for granted they may have only been or will be hand picked for you for a limited time. BeBRAVE.

BeBRAVE enough to overcome the doubt, fear, and laziness that may arise at the call of a stance.

Taking a Queen leads to being in check no matter how well you play without her.

Staying safe requires thinking. How are you thinking?

If you are a King that indulges in Queens make sure that excellences is always exude.

As a BRAVE King make sure to open your portal of mental clarity to your Queen, so that she can further indulge in her most HIGHEST form of feminine X-TACY.

As a BRAVE King it is imperative that you choose a healthy way of moving in action. Your Royalty bleeds and is VERY contagious.

Keeping the BRAVE Heart and mindset is a way of life. It's a must to hand a sacred space and spiritual practice to find your sense of calmness and PEACE.

When choosing your Queen, use the learning of yourself to gauge your complementary opposites so that your union balances out. The more you're able to absorb her feminine X-TACY and essence she is able to provide it due to the fact it's organic.

**BeBRAVE enough to allow her to use your masculinity to balance out. Make sure that you are allowing their feminine energy to charge
you as well.**

As a BRAVE King you should never fail to show up and show out when it comes to your Queen or the world. Meaning attack love and great success with your entirety. BeBRAVE in dying to ego.

As a BRAVE King never listen to the critics. Stick to your vision when the outer light gets dim. Allow that bright light within to guide your footsteps. BeBRAVE.

Enjoy your Royalty. Live as if the world is yours. If you see it and want it, make sure that it helps serve your greater purpose. Enjoy your Royalty but never take it for granted.

All of your God given powers will come effortlessly. It is up to you to notice those gifts, and
to nurture and polish them.

Through intense times make sure to always breathe. When breathing, breath fully and allow
your being to absorb and process this information in order to move forward sufficiently.

Fellow Kings are not threats. Secure your throne and the rest will be allies. Brother from another.

**All praise due to The Most High Divine Creator for THE UNITY OF THE BLACK FAMILY!!!
The Path of a JASIRI MFALME**

THE PATH OF A BRAVE KING by Alex Zackery Published by Brave Family LLC
www.bebraveattire.com

IG: @bravemoneybang

FaceBook: Alex Zackery

© 2021 The Brave Family LLC
All rights reserved. No portion of this book may be reproduced in any form without permission from the publisher, except as permitted by U.S. copyright law. For permissions contact:
bravefamily212@gmail.com
Paperback ISBN: 978-1-7368630-0-8

www.ingramcontent.com/pod-product-compliance
Lightning Source LLC
Chambersburg PA
CBHW052043220426
43663CB00012B/2428